BRICK

SEED BEAD

EARRINGS

21

PROJECTS

COLORING BOOK 3

DESIGNED BY GALIYA

 For any questions, suggestions and comments, please contact at http://www.etsy.com/shop/GaliyaDesigns

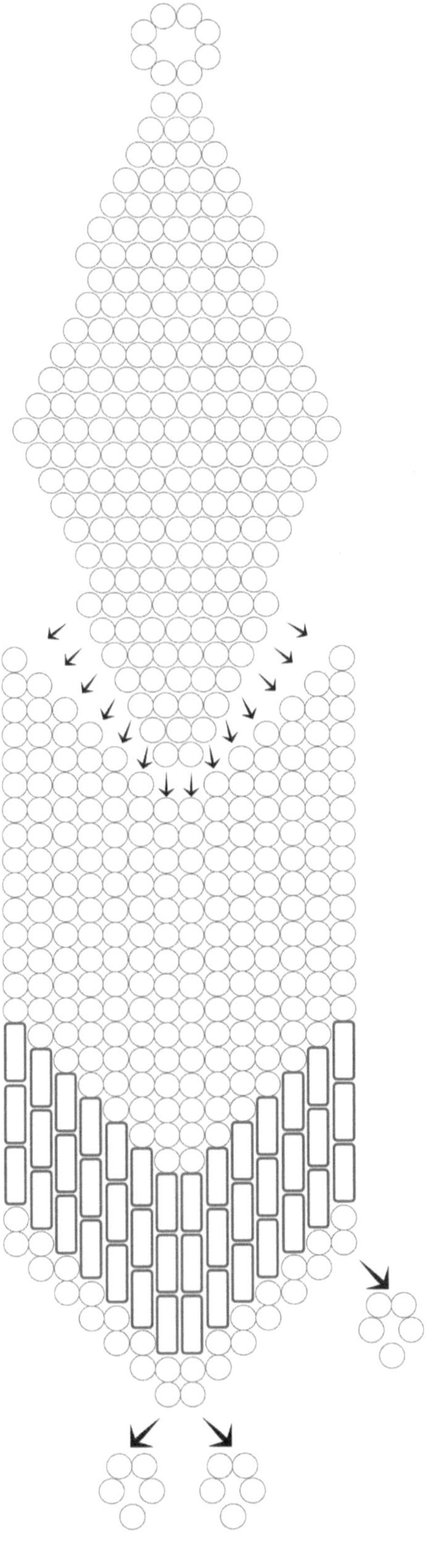

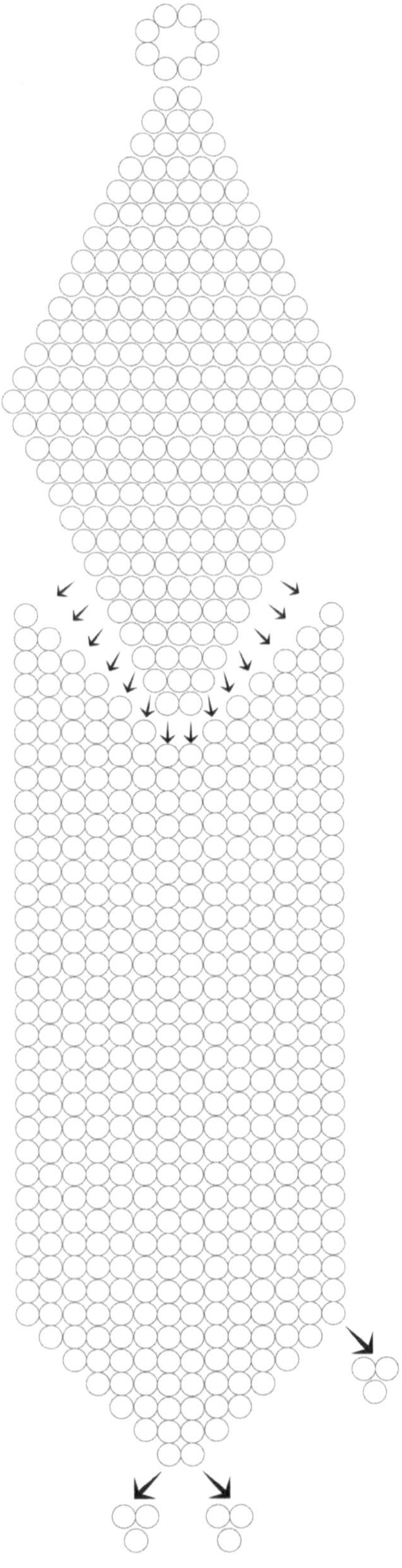

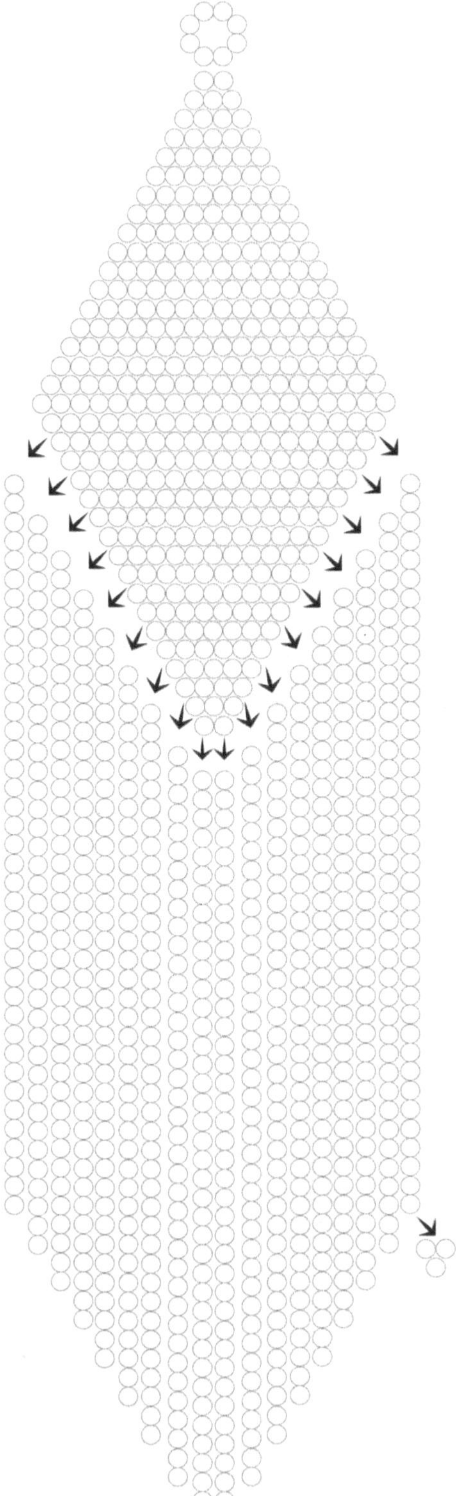

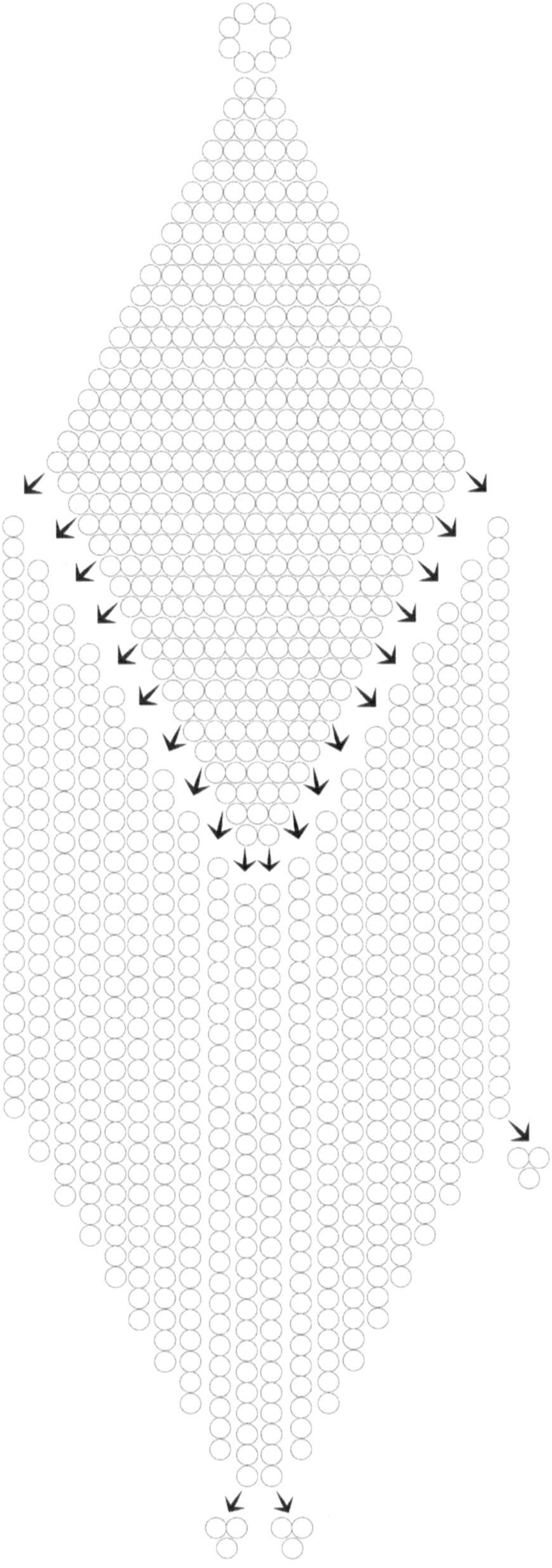

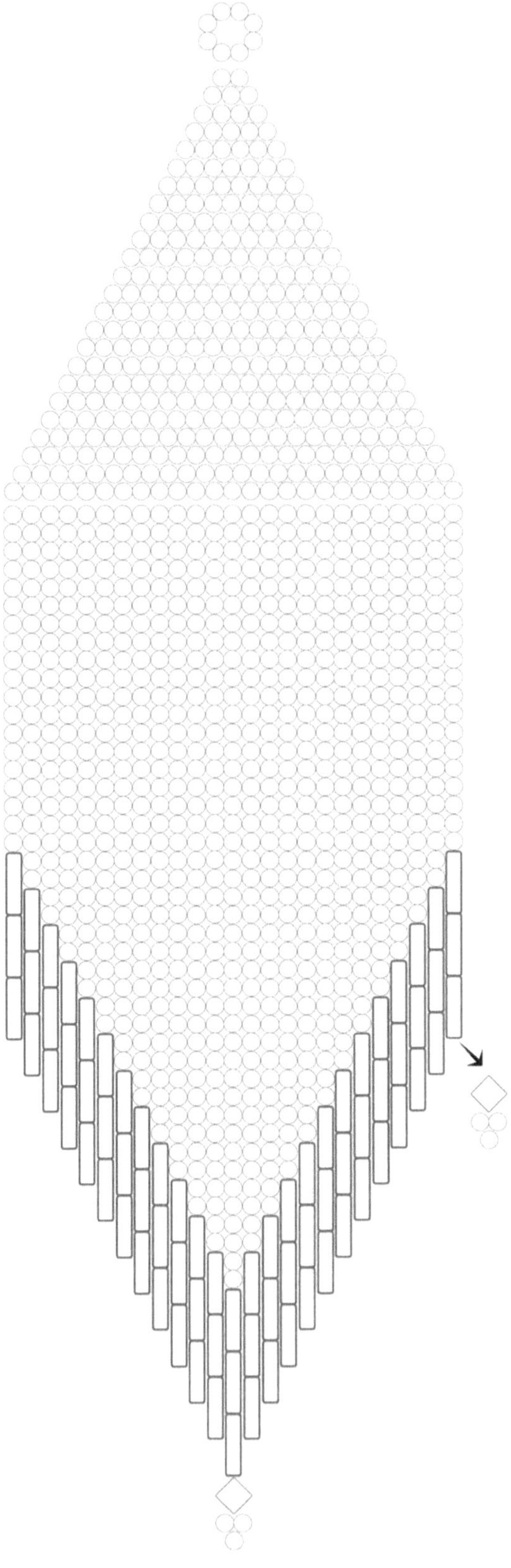

Made in United States
Troutdale, OR
07/16/2024

21255779R00030